Original title:
Chasing Starlight

Copyright © 2024 Creative Arts Management OÜ
All rights reserved.

Author: Harrison Blake
ISBN HARDBACK: 978-9916-90-586-9
ISBN PAPERBACK: 978-9916-90-587-6

Illumination Beyond the Ordinary

In shadows cast by fleeting light,
A glimmer breaks the silent night.
Each whisper glows, a soft caress,
Awakening dreams, they gently bless.

Through veils of doubt, the dawn ascends,
With every heartbeat, hope transcends.
In every glance, a spark ignites,
Transforming life into new heights.

Reflections in the Cosmos' Embrace.

Stars dance in a velvet sea,
Each twinkle tells a tale of free.
Galaxies swirl with silent grace,
Inviting hearts to find their place.

In the vastness, a soft sigh flows,
Within its depths, the universe knows.
Mirrors of light in cosmic play,
Guide our souls along the way.

Whispers of Luminescence

Upon the breeze, a secret glows,
In whispered tones, the soft light flows.
With every breath, a story spun,
Of starry nights and golden sun.

Flickering hopes in each heartbeat found,
A soft embrace, forever bound.
Radiant dreams in twilight rise,
Painting the canvas of our skies.

Celestial Echoes

In silence wrapped, the night awakes,
With every star, a longing aches.
Echoes of time in shadows play,
Marking passages in the fray.

Infinite realms in twilight's glow,
Tales of the cosmos, softly flow.
Each pulse a note in the grand design,
Harmonies lost in the divine.

Dancing in the Nebula's Embrace

In the swirl of colors bright,
Stars pulse gently, guiding light.
Whispers weave through cosmic air,
Floating softly without care.

Galaxies twirl in timeless grace,
Wrapped in warmth, a close embrace.
Stardust glimmers in our stride,
Together in this dream we glide.

Starlit Pathways

Underneath the sky's soft glow,
Winding paths where starlight flows.
Each step leads to worlds anew,
A tapestry of cosmic hue.

Footprints dance on silken beams,
Carved by hope and endless dreams.
In the night, our spirits soar,
Boundless wonders to explore.

A Dance with the Celestial

Echoes of the universe call,
In harmony, we rise and fall.
Lunar beams caress our skin,
A dance where time and space begin.

Comets whirl with fiery tails,
In this realm, our joy unveils.
With every twirl, the cosmos sings,
Uniting all with invisible strings.

The Quest for Radiant Skies

Chasing dreams through voids of night,
Hoping for a glimpse of light.
Guided by a comet's trail,
Our hearts beat strong, we shall not fail.

With every star, a story glows,
A journey where the wonder flows.
Beneath the vast, uncharted dome,
We seek the skies that call us home.

Flickers Beyond the Veil

Whispers in the twilight's gleam,
Shadows dance in silver streams.
Secrets flutter on the breeze,
Echoes of forgotten trees.

Glimmers in the afterglow,
Sending chills with tales of woe.
Flickers spark in dusky night,
Guided by the faintest light.

Formless shapes in misty air,
Luring hearts that yearn and dare.
Boundless worlds just out of sight,
With every flicker, dims the light.

Ethereal Trails

Footsteps dance on the moonlit path,
Guiding souls from shadows' wrath.
Through the mist, a breeze that calls,
Ethereal trails where silence falls.

Rippling waters softly sing,
Carried forth on night's own wing.
Floating dreams on starlit streams,
Crafted from our deepest dreams.

Segregated from the fray,
Lost in night, we drift away.
Wandering hearts bound to explore,
As ethereal trails reveal more.

Cosmic Flickers on Earth

Stars above, they shine so bright,
Winking down through velvet night.
Cosmic flickers paint the sky,
Whispers of the vastness, why?

Glimpse of realms where few can tread,
Wonders where the brave have fled.
Infinite paths intertwined,
Cosmic echoes, souls aligned.

Bursts of light from distant lands,
Connect our hopes with outstretched hands.
In the darkness, find our worth,
As we gaze at flickers on Earth.

The Allure of the Nocturnal

Underneath the silver glow,
The night unveils secrets slow.
Creatures stir in shadows deep,
Awakening from their sleep.

Wanderlust through moonlit trails,
Drifting softly, echoing tales.
The allure, it beckons near,
A world where visions reappear.

Stars conspire with the dark,
Igniting dreams to leave a mark.
In the stillness, hearts take flight,
Entranced by the charm of night.

The Allure of Aurora's Embrace

In the silence of night, colors ignite,
Waves of green dive, a celestial flight.
Whispers of magic weave through the air,
Dancing dreams blanket the world with care.

Against the chill, hearts warm with delight,
The sky paints stories in shimmering light.
Nature's tapestry, a canvas divine,
In the realm of the brave, stars intertwine.

Secrets Wrapped in Lunar Light

The moon whispers softly, secrets untold,
Casting her glow on the brave and the bold.
Shadows reveal what the daylight won't see,
Magic unfurls in the stillness, carefree.

In silver reflections, the world feels bright,
Wrapped in the comfort of lunar insight.
A journey of dreams through the night's embrace,
Where fantasies flourish in celestial grace.

Journey Through the Astral Canvas

Stars sparkle brightly, guides through the dark,
Charting the heavens, each glimmer a spark.
With every heartbeat, the cosmos awakes,
A voyage begins, with each breath it takes.

Nebulae bloom like flowers in space,
Infinite wonders in the vastness we chase.
Galaxies spin in a timeless ballet,
We dance with a hope that won't fade away.

The Dance of Distant Lights

Flickering flames in the night's gentle hush,
Stars holding secrets, in silence, they gush.
The cosmos sways with a rhythm so grand,
As dreams and desires take flight hand in hand.

Each beam tells a story, each twinkle a sound,
We gather the wishes that float all around.
In the tapestry woven by time and by fate,
We embrace the warmth of the lights that await.

Beyond the Horizon's Glitter

The waves crash with whispers soft,
As sun dips low, the dreams take flight.
Colors dance in twilight's loft,
A canvas bright, a heart so light.

Beyond where sky and ocean meet,
Adventure calls, a siren's song.
In every breeze, a tale's heartbeat,
A journey ends, yet not for long.

Luminous Trails Beneath the Skies

Stars awaken with nightly grace,
A tapestry of silver bright.
Each constellation finds its place,
Guiding souls through veils of night.

On paths of light where shadows wane,
The moon unfolds her gentle glow.
In silence echoes joy and pain,
As hearts entwine where soft winds blow.

The Quest for Ethereal Glow

In forests deep, where echoes sigh,
The whispers call from shades of green.
A flicker, a shimmer, a firefly,
Guides the dreamer, serene, unseen.

Across the fields where wildflowers grow,
Each petal holds a secret rare.
With open hearts, we seek, we know,
The magic lies in moments shared.

Midnight's Guiding Light

The clock chimes soft, the world in hush,
While shadows dance and dreams take flight.
In stillness found, in midnight's rush,
A beacon shines, a pure delight.

With every breath, the stars unfold,
A promise whispered on the breeze.
In stories told, both brave and bold,
We find our truth, our hearts at ease.

Floating in Celestial Waters

Stars shimmer softly, night unfolds,
A gentle tide, the moonlight molds.
Drift on whispers, sweet and low,
In dreams where only stardust flows.

Galaxies whisper tales of old,
Stories of love, and treasures untold.
Floating free, weightless we soar,
In celestial waters, forevermore.

Rippling reflections, dance in view,
Mirrored wonders, a world anew.
The cosmos cradles, a vast embrace,
In this timeless, enchanted space.

Beneath the vastness, hearts entwine,
Waving goodbyes to the hands of time.
Floating onward, a journey vast,
In celestial waters, our spirits cast.

Nimbus of Wandering Intent

Clouds gather thick, a stormy sigh,
Whispers of wanderers in the sky.
A nimbus forms, intent revealed,
Secrets of wanderers, fate concealed.

Swirling fog, lost in the chase,
Searching for warmth in an endless space.
With every gust, a story unfurls,
In heartbeats heard, the world swirls.

Above the treetops, dreams take flight,
Chasing the dusk into the night.
Each drop a promise, soft and true,
A gathering swell of ancient blue.

Wander we must, where spirits roam,
In nimbus veils, we find our home.
With every breath, intentions blend,
In shades of twilight, journeys mend.

The Curtain of Radiance

A veil of light, the dawn does break,
Whispers of gold, the shadows shake.
Fingers of sunlight, soft and fine,
Gently dance on the edge of time.

Colors burst forth, vibrant and clear,
The world's awakening, sweet and near.
A curtain drawn, revealing the day,
In every ray, our worries sway.

Hearts ignite in the morning's glow,
Promises made in the light's flow.
With each step, the brightness sings,
A tapestry woven from golden strings.

The curtain of radiance, love's embrace,
Fills every corner, each sacred space.
In the warmth of this dazzling art,
We find the light that ignites the heart.

Footsteps on Lunar Dust

Silvery plains beneath our feet,
Lunar whispers, the night is sweet.
Every footprint tells a tale,
Of cosmic ships and a dreamer's sail.

Stars gaze down with a knowing glance,
In the silence, we begin to dance.
Each heartbeat echoes, soft and slow,
Guided by moonlight's gentle glow.

Shadows linger where dreams reside,
In a cradle of wonder, we confide.
With every breath, we rise and fall,
Embracing the magic, answering the call.

Footsteps on dust, a journey grand,
In the vastness, we take a stand.
Together we wander, the night our guide,
On lunar paths, where dreams abide.

Lost in the Constellation's Maze

In shadows of the night we roam,
Stars whisper secrets, calling us home.
Galaxies twist, a celestial embrace,
We wander the paths, lost in time and space.

Navigating dreams with footprints of light,
Chasing the echoes that fade out of sight.
Constellations flicker, like eyes from afar,
Guiding our hearts through the dark, like a star.

The Promise of Celestial Wanderings

Beyond the horizon where dreams take flight,
Lies a promise born of the endless night.
Planets and moons in harmonious dance,
Every heartbeat fueled by the wild expanse.

Through cosmic tides, our spirits ascend,
Chasing the visions that never quite end.
In the void, we find our wishes unfurled,
Connected as one, in this vast, starry world.

In Search of Elysian Beacons

We seek the glow of the Elysian lights,
To guide us through life, in its darkest nights.
With fragile hands, we reach for the grace,
Of fleeting moments, time cannot trace.

In whispers of stardust, our hopes are spun,
Under the gaze of a thousand suns.
Drawing us closer, the beacons will shine,
Illuminating paths intertwined in design.

Skimming the Surface of Infinity

Like waves on an ocean, we drift and glide,
Awash in the currents where mysteries hide.
A dance with the cosmos, so graceful and free,
In the tapestry woven of you and me.

We skim through the moments, ephemeral dreams,
Reflecting the light in a million beams.
In the shimmer of stars, our souls intertwine,
Forever in flow, like the paths of divine.

Stardust Secrets

Whispers of stars in the velvet sky,
Dance with the winds as they fleetingly sigh.
Each spark a story, a moment in time,
Spinning the cosmos in rhythms and rhyme.

Galaxies twinkle, their secrets unfold,
Tales of the ancients in light-years untold.
The night is alive with celestial dreams,
Where stardust ignites and imagination beams.

In silence they speak, the hermit of space,
Guiding the lost to a safer embrace.
Caught in their brilliance, the heart can't resist,
For each glowing point holds a precious wish.

So gather the wishes, release them in flight,
Let stardust secrets illuminate the night.
With every breath, feel the magic increase,
As dreams born of cosmos bring infinite peace.

Hallowed Be the Night

In shadows deep where whispers dwell,
The night enfolds its sacred spell.
Stars twinkle softly, a dimming light,
Hallowed be the calm of the night.

Moonlit paths weave tales untold,
Guardians of dreams with hearts of gold.
Embrace the dark where secrets lie,
In silence, the world lets out a sigh.

Gentle breezes carry the tunes,
Of soft lullabies beneath the moons.
Each moment cherished, a treasure bright,
As the universe cradles our plight.

So bow to the night and listen close,
For in its embrace, the spirits do boast.
Hallowed be the time when we unite,
In the stillness, we find our light.

The Allure of Distant Dreams

Across the horizon, where hopes take flight,
Wander the realms, bathed in twilight.
Distant dreams beckon, their whispers sweet,
With promise of journeys, new paths to greet.

In starlit skies, they shimmer and glow,
Inviting the restless to follow and go.
Each vision a tapestry, vivid and grand,
Woven together by fate's gentle hand.

Through valleys of shadow, on mountains so high,
A tapestry woven beneath the vast sky.
The allure ignites the most yearning souls,
To chase every dream where the heart feels whole.

So let imagination take lead in the dance,
For distant dreams offer a chance to enhance.
With every heartbeat they come alive,
In the fabric of night, our spirits thrive.

Voyage of the Night Scavenger

Under the cloak of the ink-black skies,
The night scavenger stirs, where shadows lie.
Cloaked in the moonlight, they wander and roam,
Seeking out treasures that mirror their home.

The rustle of leaves, the whispers of air,
Each secret in darkness, the scavenger's fare.
With sharpened senses, they roam without fear,
In search of the echoes that the shadows near.

From starlit dreams to forgotten old tales,
The keeper of secrets where magic prevails.
In every lost moment, a story they find,
Binding together the threads of mankind.

So watch as they glide through the quivering night,
For the night scavenger dances with light.
In the depth of the dark, adventures ignite,
And dreams become real in their journey through night.

Twilight's Hidden Wonders

In shadows deep, the secrets dwell,
Where whispers of the night can tell.
A fleeting glow, a firefly's dance,
In twilight's embrace, we find our chance.

The stars unveil their hidden grace,
As darkness drapes the world's embrace.
The moon, a guardian watching still,
Awakens dreams, ignites the will.

The Symphony of Distant Stars

In silence, echoes from afar,
The symphony of each bright star.
They twinkle softly, tales untold,
A cosmic choir in night's hold.

In harmony, the galaxies spin,
A rhythmic dance where dreams begin.
Together woven, light's refrain,
The universe sings, and we remain.

Caught in Cosmic Currents

Drifting through the velvet night,
Caught in currents of pure light.
Galactic winds, they pull us near,
To places woven in the sphere.

In stellar streams, we find our path,
A cosmic flow, we feel its wrath.
Yet in the midst, we find our grace,
As we embrace this endless space.

Unraveling the Universe's Veil

A tapestry of time and space,
We seek the secrets, trace their place.
Each thread reveals a world anew,
As wonders wait for hearts so true.

With every glance, the cosmos stirs,
Unraveling what time prefers.
In starlit whispers, we connect,
The universe holds us in respect.

Wanderlust Amongst the Stars

In the still of night, I roam wide,
A canvas of dreams, where hopes abide.
With each twinkling light, my heart shall soar,
The whispers of distance call for more.

Across cosmic seas, my spirit glides,
Through constellations, where secrets reside.
In search of the worlds, both near and far,
Wanderlust ignites, a guiding star.

I dance with the shadows, bathed in glow,
Each pulse of the cosmos, a tale to bestow.
Endless horizons, where wonders align,
Forever I'll chase, the divine design.

With stardust in hand, I journey on,
Charting my path till the break of dawn.
In the embrace of night, I find my way,
Wanderlust among the stars shall sway.

Embracing the Celestial Chase

Beneath the vastness, the night unfolds,
The universe beckons with stories untold.
I run with the comets, swift and free,
Embracing the chase, just my dreams and me.

The moon, my companion, whispers sweet,
Carving out paths where the stardust meets.
In the quiet of space, I feel the pull,
Of mysteries swirling, enchantingly full.

Galaxies spin in a delicate dance,
With every heartbeat, I seize my chance.
Each nebula glimmers, a spark in the night,
As I wander through realms of shimmering light.

With courage ignited, I take to the skies,
Chasing horizons where wonder lies.
In the tapestry woven by stars up above,
I find my journey, my passion, my love.

A Tapestry of Night and Bright

Intricate threads of night and bright,
Woven in shadows, kissed by light.
A symphony of silence, the moon's soft glow,
Guides the heart where the wild dreams flow.

Each star a story, a voice from the past,
Echoes of ages where time holds fast.
In the quilt of the cosmos, we find our place,
A tapestry stitched with celestial grace.

Through velvet skies, we drift and weave,
Gathering hopes that the stars believe.
An endless expanse, where wishes ignite,
In the mystery wrapped by the blanket of night.

I long for the moments when all is still,
To chase after echoes, to feel the thrill.
In this cosmic dance, I shall forever roam,
Amongst the wonders that call me home.

Reveries Beneath the Starry Canopy

Under the canopy, dreams take flight,
Bathed in the glow of a thousand lights.
Soft whispers of wisdom drift with the breeze,
As I ponder the secrets of stars with ease.

The night cradles tales of forgotten time,
In echoes of starlight, a tranquil rhyme.
With every heartbeat, I muse and sigh,
In reveries woven, our spirits fly high.

From dusk till the dawn, I wander and gaze,
In the stillness of night, lost in a haze.
The cosmos expands, a sea of delight,
As I delve into magic, enshrined in the night.

Surrounded by wonders, I find my peace,
Embracing the stillness, my soul's release.
Each moment a treasure, forever it lasts,
In reveries below, where my heart is cast.

The Chase for Shimmering Horizons

Across the fields where wildflowers sway,
The sun dips low, kissed by the day.
Chasing dreams as they fade from sight,
We run together, hearts burning bright.

The horizon calls with a whispered plea,
A promise of worlds that we long to see.
With every step, the thrill ignites,
In this dance of shadows, our future lights.

Clouds painted gold by the setting sun,
We leap for joy as the race is won.
In the twilight glow, our spirits soar,
Together we find what we longed for.

Through valleys deep to mountains high,
We chase the stars in a velvet sky.
With each heartbeat, we redefine fate,
In the chase for horizons, we resonate.

Celestial Footprints

Under the moon, the world stands still,
Footprints in stardust, a gentle thrill.
Whispers of cosmos, secrets untold,
Guiding our journey, courageous and bold.

The night unveils a magical map,
With every step, we draw a new gap.
Stars wink at us, like old friends near,
In this celestial dance, we conquer fear.

The constellations twinkle and sway,
Marking our passage through night and day.
With hearts united, we roam far and wide,
Celestial footprints, our souls as guide.

Together we wander, together we dream,
In the embrace of night, we endlessly gleam.
These footprints linger in the sky's vast sea,
A testament to love, forever we'll be.

Hues of the Night's Tapestry

The canvas of night, a tapestry spun,
Hues intermingling, dusk's art begun.
Whispers of color blend deep and bright,
Painting our dreams in the cloak of night.

Silver and indigo, shadows entwine,
A symphony of shades, so wondrously fine.
We trace the edges of twilight's grace,
Finding our peace in this sacred space.

Stars emerge as the daylight fades,
Threads of golden light, where hope cascades.
In the cool embrace of the night's soft fall,
We find our voices, we hear the call.

With laughter and love, our spirits ignite,
In the hues of the night, everything feels right.
Binding our hearts in this magical view,
The tapestry of dreams, forever imbued.

Embracing the Twilight's Magic

As daylight whispers its sweet goodbye,
Twilight descends with a gentle sigh.
The air is charged with a shimmering glow,
Inviting us deeper, where mysteries flow.

The stars awaken, one by one,
In the soft embrace of a day just done.
We gather moments like petals around,
In twilight's magic, our dreams are found.

Soft shadows dance with the fading light,
Leading us onward, setting hearts alight.
With hands entwined, we cherish the hour,
Under the spell of the night's soft power.

Embracing the twilight, we breathe in the grace,
Painting our memories in this sacred space.
Together we wander, lost in its charm,
In twilight's magic, we find our warm.

A Dance Beneath the Cosmic Glow

Underneath the starlit sky,
Whispers of the night draw near.
Swirling lights begin to fly,
Carried by the gentle sphere.

With each step, the shadows sway,
The world is hushed, so still, so bright.
Moonlight guides us on our way,
As we dance into the night.

Colors blend, a vivid stream,
In the quiet, spirits play.
Held within this fleeting dream,
Forever in the stars we stay.

With every twirl, a heartbeat sings,
Echoes of the heavens' tune.
Through the dark, our laughter rings,
Dancing 'neath the silver moon.

Echoes of the Night's Radiance

In the dark, the stars ignite,
Whispers float upon the breeze.
Guided by the soft moonlight,
Echoes dance through ancient trees.

Silver beams on faces shine,
Casting shadows, soft and low.
Crickets chirp in rhythmic line,
Nature's symphony in flow.

Lost in thoughts of dreams untold,
Every sparkle sparks a thought.
Stories woven, treasures bold,
Within the night, the heart is caught.

Mysterious, the silence speaks,
Secrets shared 'neath glowing light.
In the calm, the magic peaks,
Echoes weave through the night.

Threads of Silver in Midnight's Veil

Beneath the canvas of the night,
Silver threads begin to weave.
In the dark, a gentle light,
Shimmers soft for those who believe.

Whispers caught in shadows play,
Dancing dreams upon the ground.
Every heartbeat leads the way,
Near the stars, we become unbound.

With each breath, the cosmos sings,
Songs of love and hope entwined.
In the vastness, freedom clings,
Embraced by night, the world aligned.

Underneath the velvet skies,
Threads of silver tail the night.
In their glow, the spirit flies,
Wrapped in dreams, we find our light.

The Pathway of Shimmering Dreams

On the pathway lined with stars,
Shimmering dreams begin to glow.
Guided by the light from afar,
Finding treasures in the flow.

Each step forward, echoes call,
Filling hearts with whispers sweet.
In the silence, shadows fall,
Where the night and starlight meet.

As we wander, hand in hand,
Through the labyrinth of the night.
We create our own wonderland,
Painting visions, pure delight.

In the tapestry of time,
Dreams will dance and softly gleam.
Together, we will climb and climb,
Along the path of every dream.

Flickering Hopes in the Dark

In shadows deep, where silence breathes,
A whisper stirs, a flicker weaves.
Through tangled dreams and fragile sighs,
Hope rises gently, like dawn in the skies.

Each heartbeat holds a flicker fair,
A flame that dances in the air.
With every tear, a spark ignites,
Illuminating the lonely nights.

Beneath the weight of endless fears,
A lantern glows through all the tears.
In darkest hours, we'll find our way,
With flickering hopes to guide the stray.

So let us tread this path anew,
With courage forged and spirits true.
For in the night, together we'll shine,
As flickering hopes through shadows align.

Embrace of the Radiant Horizon

Where sun meets sea, in hues so bright,
The horizon whispers, day turns to night.
With arms outstretched, we greet the day,
In colors bold, we lose our way.

The golden rays, a warm embrace,
A dance of light, a sacred space.
With every step, the world unfolds,
In vibrant shades, our dreams are bold.

As shadows fall and twilight sighs,
The stars emerge in evening skies.
We count the glimmers, one by one,
In the embrace of the setting sun.

In every heartbeat, a radiant beat,
We chase the horizon, never retreat.
With hope as our guide, we sail afar,
To the embrace of each radiant star.

Glimmers in the Velvet Abyss

In the abyss where shadows weave,
Glimmers dance and softly cleave.
A tapestry of silent grace,
In velvet dark, we find our place.

Each twinkle holds a story dear,
Of hopes entwined, of whispered fear.
Through depths unknown, the light will steer,
Guiding souls that wander near.

The velvet night, a cloak divine,
Wraps us close with threads of time.
In every glimmer, a spark awaits,
To light the path through hidden gates.

So let us wander, hand in hand,
Through the abyss, a glittering land.
For in the dark, our hearts will glow,
With glimmers bright that lovingly flow.

Songs from the Edge of the Universe

Beyond the stars, a song does rise,
In cosmic winds where silence lies.
Notes of starlight, soft and clear,
Whisper to the hearts that hear.

From distant worlds, a melody spills,
Carried on the ether's thrills.
In every note, a tale unfolds,
Of mysteries deep and wonders bold.

The edge of night, a choir sings,
Of dreams that soar on radiant wings.
With every echo, time stands still,
In the universe, we find our thrill.

So listen closely, let it be,
The songs of space, wild and free.
They call to us, through light and dark,
Songs from the edge, igniting the spark.

Lanterns in the Infinite Sky

Little lights flicker bright,
They dance with the stars at night.
Whispers of dreams take flight,
Guiding souls with pure delight.

Gentle wind carries tales,
Of love and hope that never pales.
In the silence, joy prevails,
Beneath the moon, the heart exhales.

Galaxies spin, a cosmic show,
Each lantern's glow, a secret flow.
Messages from long ago,
In the night's embrace, we grow.

As the dawn begins to break,
The lanterns fade, but hearts awake.
In their memory, dreams we stake,
In the infinite sky, the bonds we make.

Beyond the Twilight Border

Shadows linger, soft and deep,
In twilight's grasp, the world will weep.
Colors blend, in silence steep,
Beyond the border, secrets keep.

Dreamers walk with hearts aglow,
Through fields where wildflowers grow.
Each petal whispers tales of woe,
And hopes that shimmer, ebb and flow.

The stars emerge, a guiding light,
Leading souls through the velvet night.
In the distance, echoes bright,
Beyond the twilight, hearts take flight.

With each step toward the dawn,
The shadows fade, the worries gone.
In the warmth of a new day's yawn,
We find ourselves, reborn, drawn.

Reflections on Starlit Waters

Underneath the moon's soft gaze,
Waters shimmer in gentle ways.
Reflections of the nights ablaze,
Where dreams drift in quiet phase.

Ripples tell of tales unfurled,
In the stillness, magic swirled.
Starlit secrets slowly hurled,
Within the depths, a hidden world.

Echoes dance on the surface bare,
Drawing whispers from the air.
Each reflection a secret dare,
A glimpse of wonders, pure and rare.

As dawn approaches, shadows flee,
Leaving only what's meant to be.
In the heart of the deep blue sea,
We find our truth, forever free.

Surrender to the Cosmic Tide

Waves crash softly on the shore,
Carrying dreams forevermore.
In the ebb and flow, we explore,
Surrendering, we find the core.

Stars above, a vast expanse,
Inviting us to take a chance.
In the tides, life's endless dance,
A cosmic journey, a sacred trance.

Let go of fears, embrace the ride,
With open hearts, the world's our guide.
In the darkness, let love abide,
Surrender to the cosmic tide.

As we drift in celestial sea,
Unified, we will always be.
In the depths of infinity,
We find our place, wild and free.

Ribbons of Radiance

In the dawn, the colors play,
Ribbons of light chase night away.
Soft whispers through the morning breeze,
Nature's canvas, a sight that frees.

Golden hues in a sky so vast,
Each moment fleeting, gone so fast.
Fingers of sun touch the earth,
Awakening dreams, igniting worth.

Petals open to greet the day,
In graceful arcs, they sway and sway.
The world catches fire, alive with grace,
In each heartbeat, time finds its place.

A tapestry woven with delicate threads,
Casting shadows where the light spreads.
In this moment, the heart takes flight,
Ribbons of radiance, pure delight.

Nightfall's Serenade

As the sun dips below the hill,
Stars awaken, the air is still.
Moonlight dances on tranquil waves,
In the night, the heart behaves.

Crickets sing their soft refrain,
Echoes of joy mingled with pain.
A silken breeze whispers secrets low,
Underneath the celestial glow.

Shadows stretch with a gentle sigh,
While the night swathes the world in nigh.
Each breath a story, rich and wide,
In the dark, our dreams confide.

The universe hums its ancient tune,
Carried softly by the silver moon.
In the stillness, we find our place,
Nightfall's serenade, a sweet embrace.

In Pursuit of Cosmic Whispers

Beyond the stars where silence reigns,
In pursuit of whispers, the soul gains.
Galaxies twirl in a dance of night,
Echoing secrets, hidden from sight.

Dreamers seek in the vast unknown,
Yearning for truths that can't be shown.
Every heartbeat pulses with light,
Guiding the way through the infinite night.

Celestial songs weave through the dark,
Filling the void with a radiant spark.
In stillness, the universe breathes deep,
Secrets of ages no one can keep.

With open hearts, we chase the dark,
For cosmic whispers ignite the spark.
In pursuit of the vast and the free,
We find ourselves in eternity.

The Lure of the Infinite

Across the void where dreams collide,
The lure of the infinite calls us wide.
Endless horizons beckon the brave,
In the depths of the cosmos, we crave.

Vastness stretches, a canvas so grand,
Mysterious forces we strive to understand.
Through galaxies where starlight weaves,
The heart of creation quietly breathes.

Each voyage a dance of time and space,
We seek the wonders that time can't erase.
In the arms of the cosmos, we find our way,
The lure of the infinite, night and day.

With every step, the journey unfolds,
Tales of eternity waiting to be told.
Together we wander, forever to roam,
In the arms of the infinite, we find a home.

Navigating the Sea of Stars

In the hush of twilight's glow,
I set my sail to the unknown.
Waves of light dance above,
Guiding me to realms unknown.

Each twinkle whispers a tale,
Of journeys past and dreams anew.
The vast expanse calls to me,
As I chart my course through the blue.

Constellations map the night,
Celestial guides of ancient lore.
With every star, I find my way,
Across the cosmic ocean's floor.

A mariner of dreams, I roam,
Through the velvet fabric of night.
With every breath, I feel alive,
In the starry sea, my heart takes flight.

Lured by the Celestial Phosphorescence

A glow from depths I can't ignore,
Pulling me closer to the shore.
The night air hums with life,
As cosmic wonders start to soar.

Phosphorescent waves, they shine,
Like secrets whispered in the dark.
Each ripple tells of distant realms,
Igniting dreams with every spark.

In this dance of light and shade,
I lose myself to starlit bliss.
The universe beckons wide,
With promises in every kiss.

Caught in the tide of glowing dreams,
I drift through worlds beyond my view.
With the night sky as my guide,
I chase the wonders, ever true.

The Fabric of Night Illuminated

The night unfolds in draped shadows,
Woven threads of silver and gold.
Stars stitch patterns of the past,
As mysteries of ages unfold.

Dreams hang like lanterns aglow,
Illuminating paths ahead.
Through darkened lanes, I wander free,
Where tales of starlight gently spread.

The fabric of night, rich and deep,
Weaves stories of hope and fear.
With each twinkle, a heartbeat's pulse,
A lullaby only the night can hear.

Among the constellations bright,
I find pieces of my soul's delight.
The cosmos whispers in soft tones,
Wrapping me in the warmth of night.

Starlit Dreams and Wandering Wishes

Beneath the stars, I close my eyes,
Wishes float on midnight air.
Starlit dreams weave through my mind,
Taking flight without a care.

Each wish a beacon shining bright,
Illuminating hopes untold.
With the galaxy as my stage,
I dance with dreams both brave and bold.

Wandering through cosmic realms,
I grasp at moments made of light.
In this celestial tapestry,
I collect my dreams each night.

Echoes of my heart's desire,
Echo within the astral glow.
Starlit dreams and wandering wishes,
Together in the night, we flow.

Enchanted by the Edges of Night

The moon hangs low in velvet sky,
Whispers of twilight gently sigh.
Shadows dance beneath the trees,
As stars awaken with a breeze.

Crickets chirp their soft refrain,
Echoing dreams that leave a stain.
Night's embrace so warm and deep,
Calls the wanderers from their sleep.

With silver beams that gently glow,
Magic flourishes, hearts aglow.
In celestial silence, we find,
The secrets of our troubled mind.

Oh, how the edges softly gleam,
We lose ourselves within a dream.
As darkness wraps around us tight,
We are enchanted by the night.

Fragments of Astral Wonder

Glittering shards in cosmic spray,
Dance through the night, they whirl and sway.
Each twinkle holds a story bright,
In the depths of eternal night.

Galaxies weave a tapestry,
Fragments of dreams, wild and free.
Stars shimmer with ancient grace,
A boundless expanse, a timeless space.

Planets spin in rhythmic flight,
Guided by a celestial light.
Each breath of wind, a cosmic tide,
Through the universe, we glide.

Lost in the beauty of the vast,
Wondering if we could hold fast.
To fragments shimmering above,
Whispers of the universe, love.

Enigmas of the Heavenly Dance

Celestial bodies whirl and twirl,
In patterns that make the universe swirl.
A ballet of shadows in the night,
Enigmas wrapped in pure delight.

Constellations tell tales of old,
In the silence, their stories unfold.
Each heartbeat syncs to the cosmic song,
In rhythms where we all belong.

Dancing with grace, a timeless flow,
The mysteries of night softly glow.
We move through this celestial trance,
Awakening dreams in a cosmic dance.

Every star a step we take,
In the vastness, our spirits awake.
The heavenly dance never ends,
In the night, our spirit transcends.

Where Stars Whisper Secrets

In the quiet of the midnight hour,
Stars reveal their hidden power.
They whisper secrets, soft and low,
Guiding the lost with golden glow.

Across the sky, a tapestry bright,
Veils of wonder, a mystical sight.
Each flicker, a promise, a prayer,
In the silence, we stop and stare.

Dreams are woven in starlit thread,
A cosmic dreamscape where few dare tread.
With every breath, we draw them near,
In the stillness, we silence fear.

So let the night cradle your soul,
With stars that make the broken whole.
In this realm where whispers blend,
We find the secrets that never end.

Slipstream of the Nebula

In the vastness where stars collide,
Colors dance in cosmic tide.
Whispers of light weave through the dark,
Each heartbeat ignites a spark.

Galaxies swirl in a timeless embrace,
Tracing the paths of an endless chase.
Nebulas cradle the dreams of old,
Through slipstreams of stardust, stories unfold.

Fragments of comets, a shimmering trail,
Eons lost in the cosmic scale.
As celestial winds carry the night,
Hope finds a way in the fading light.

Awash in a sea of glowing dust,
In the universe, we place our trust.
Each moment a note in this grand symphony,
Together, we drift in eternal harmony.

Navigating the Celestial Sea

Sailing towards the moons aglow,
Stars our compass as we flow.
Constellations whisper with grace,
Guiding us through the vast space.

Waves of light ripple through time,
Every pulse a silent rhyme.
In the depths of the night's veil,
Ancient tales begin to sail.

Celestial wonders unfold on high,
As we chart the secrets of the sky.
Navigating dreams on a cosmic quest,
Finding solace in the universe's chest.

With every twinkle, a wish takes flight,
Writing our hopes in the silver light.
Together we wander, forever true,
In cosmic waters, me and you.

Night's Hidden Labyrinth

In shadows deep, the secrets lie,
Whispers surround as the night draws nigh.
A maze of starlight, winding and bright,
Guiding lost souls through endless night.

Every turn a story to unbind,
In the labyrinth where dreams unwind.
Echoes of laughter, forgotten fears,
Lost in the passage of timeless years.

Moonlight filters through tangled dreams,
Painting paths with silvery beams.
Each misstep brings a new surprise,
Echoing truths in the midnight skies.

Finding beauty in the dark's embrace,
In the hidden corners of this place.
Together we seek what the night conceals,
In the labyrinth, our fate reveals.

The Glow of Forgotten Dreams

In twilight's grasp, shadows recede,
Echoes of wishes plant their seed.
Flickers of hope in the somber light,
Whispers of dreams take their flight.

Years may fade, but embers remain,
Tracing the path of joy and pain.
Each spark a reminder of what was tried,
In the chambers where longing resides.

The glow of the past bathes us anew,
In the warmth of solace, we gather our crew.
Chasing the shadows with laughter and song,
Finding our way where we all belong.

Hand in hand, we embrace the glow,
In the tapestry of life, we sow.
For in forgotten dreams, we find our way,
Guided by starlight, forever we stray.

Reverie in the Night

In shadows deep, the whispers sigh,
Moonlit dreams begin to fly.
Stars cascade, a shimmering lace,
Guiding thoughts to a tranquil space.

In the hush of dusk they gleam,
Softly weaving a quiet scheme.
Each twinkle holds a secret bright,
Enticing hearts in the still of night.

Drifting through the realms of time,
Painting memories, oh so sublime.
Liquid silver, thoughts take flight,
Capturing echoes of pure delight.

Awake within this gentle trance,
As starlit visions weave and dance.
In the reverie, we find our way,
Guided by night, till break of day.

Journey to the Cosmic Glimmer

Across the skies, I chart my course,
Riding waves of a starlit force.
In the vastness, wonders bloom,
Each spark ignites, banishing gloom.

Galaxies swirl in a cosmic embrace,
Whispers of time in endless space.
With every pulse, I feel the call,
A timeless dance, a celestial thrall.

Boundless dreams stretch far and wide,
With constellations as my guide.
Floating softly, I take my flight,
Towards the glow of the distant light.

Journey onward, where dreams ignite,
With cosmic glimmers, hearts unite.
Through the darkness, we shine so bright,
Together chasing the endless night.

Threads of Astral Dreams

Woven softly in starlit seams,
Threads of gold in astral dreams.
Each whisper carried on a breeze,
Entwined in tales that gently tease.

Mending souls with cosmic grace,
In the fabric of time and space.
Cloth of wonders, colors blend,
A tapestry where lives transcend.

In far-off realms, where shadows play,
I trace the paths, let spirits sway.
Each woven strand, a story told,
Of wandering hearts, both brave and bold.

As night departs, dreams linger near,
With threads of light, we hold what's dear.
In the silence, our hopes gleam bright,
Stitched together by the hands of night.

Pursuit of the Guiding Lights

In the depths of darkness, we seek the glow,
Guiding lights that softly show.
They flicker gently, a beckoning call,
Leading lost souls, one and all.

With every step, we chase the beam,
Fueled by hope, igniting dreams.
The path unfolds, night's secrets blend,
In the pursuit, our hearts transcend.

Each star a promise, a map to trace,
Illuminating every hidden place.
Whether near or far, we're drawn to shine,
With guiding lights, our spirits align.

Together, we rise, unbroken flight,
In pursuit of wisdom, love, and light.
Across the heavens, we find our way,
Chasing the dawn, till break of day.

Echoes of the Unseen

In shadows deep, whispers roam,
Beneath the skin, they find a home.
Silent tales the night reveals,
Voices lost that presence steals.

Ghostly footfalls through the air,
Memories drift without a care.
In the quiet, secrets wait,
Echoes thrum, but hesitate.

Behind closed eyes, they softly speak,
In every glance and every peak.
The past collides with what may be,
A haunting dance, eternally.

In whispered dreams, we tread with grace,
Finding solace in empty space.
An unseen world, we hold so dear,
Echoes sing, yet few can hear.

Traces of Ethereal Glow

Amidst the dusk, a shimmer shines,
Softly tracing ancient lines.
Flickers dance on twilight's seam,
In every heart, a hidden dream.

Golden threads weave through the night,
Stars awaken, burning bright.
Underneath the cosmic dome,
A gentle pull, a sense of home.

Waves of light in silence flow,
Kissing edges where shadows grow.
Voices of the past emerge,
A symphony, a vivid surge.

In the dark, their secrets wait,
Whispers echo, contemplate.
Ethereal hands, they guide us slow,
Tracing paths in the afterglow.

Wanderlust Among the Constellations

Beneath the stars, my heart takes flight,
Chasing dreams across the night.
Endless skies that call my name,
Each star a spark, igniting flame.

Across the vast, I wander free,
Mapping constellations' decree.
In their glow, I find my way,
Lost and found, come what may.

Galaxies hold stories untold,
Whispers of the brave and bold.
Every twinkle, a siren's sound,
In their depths, my soul is found.

Through cosmic dance, I roam afar,
Guided by the light of stars.
Wanderlust through skies so wide,
Among the constellations, I reside.

Lightyear Longing

In the fabric of the night,
Distance wears a cloak of light.
Lightyears stretch but cannot hide,
The yearning that beats inside.

Across the void, where silence reigns,
Hearts entwined, love never wanes.
A universe of dreams to share,
Longing whispers through the air.

Time defies, yet feels so near,
In the stars, I see you clear.
Each pulse of light a glowing trace,
Drawing me toward your embrace.

Though time may move and space may bend,
My thoughts to you shall never end.
Through galaxies, my heart takes flight,
In lightyear longing, love ignites.

Navigating by Flickering Light

In the dark where shadows play,
Stars are whispers, soft and gray.
With every flicker, dreams take flight,
Guiding hearts through endless night.

A lantern's glow, a path unfolds,
Hope ignited, courage bold.
Step by step on this lonely road,
Trust the light to share the load.

Moments fade, but sparks remain,
Embers dance in joy and pain.
Flickering flames of tales retold,
In dreams alive, we find the gold.

So wander forth, embrace the dark,
Let every flicker leave a mark.
As shadows stretch and night takes flight,
We'll find our way by flickering light.

The Compass of the Night Sky

Underneath this endless dome,
Stars align, a guide to roam.
A compass drawn with silver trails,
In the night where wonder sails.

Celestial maps, a treasure sought,
In every twinkle, lessons taught.
Navigating through the maze,
Of memories lost in twilight haze.

Constellations, stories spun,
A cosmic dance, we're all as one.
With every step, the dawn will break,
Unraveling the paths we make.

So cast your gaze, let spirits fly,
Trust the compass of the night sky.
In starlit dreams, we'll forge our way,
Forever guided, come what may.

Silhouettes Under Astral Rain

Beneath the sky, a canvas painted,
Silhouettes in shadows fainted.
Dancing drops of light cascade,
Whispers soft of dreams mislaid.

In the night, we weave our fate,
Beneath the stars, we contemplate.
Astral rain, a gentle touch,
Fills our hearts, we long for much.

Figures move in a balmy breeze,
Lost in thought, with quiet ease.
Unseen threads connect our souls,
In the dark, where magic rolls.

So let the night embrace our fears,
In shadows deep, we shed our tears.
Underneath this astral rain,
We'll find our peace amidst the pain.

Illuminated By Dreaming

In whispers soft, the night appears,
Our dreams take flight, allay our fears.
Beneath the stars, our visions glow,
A tapestry of hope we sew.

Awake we drift through realms unknown,
Where twilight's magic gently shone.
Each thought a spark, a guiding light,
Illuminating paths of night.

Through shadows deep, our spirits soar,
With every heartbeat, we explore.
In slumber's arms, we find our way,
To brighter places, come what may.

Together lost in starlit schemes,
In every heart, a world of dreams.
The night unfolds its ancient grace,
Inviting us to find our place.

Starlit Journeys of the Heart

Beneath the sky, so vast and wide,
Our hearts embark, our fears subside.
With every step, the cosmos gleams,
On starlit paths, we chase our dreams.

Through galaxies, our spirits glide,
In every twinkle, love's confide.
Each heartbeat echoes in the dark,
As we traverse the endless arc.

The silence sings, the shadows dance,
In every glance, we find romance.
Together, we embrace the night,
With cosmic kisses, pure delight.

In unison, our hearts will roam,
Across the stars, we find our home.
With every journey, love will spark,
In starlit travels, we leave our mark.

Galactic Reveries

In gamma rays, our dreams ignite,
A galaxy born of pure delight.
Stars whisper secrets, softly spun,
In cosmic tales, our lives are run.

Dark matter holds our hopes and fears,
As black holes cradle lost goodbyes.
A cosmic dance of time and space,
In this vast sea, we find our grace.

Clad in the night, we wander free,
Through supernovas, our hearts decree.
In radiant hues, our spirits blend,
Together we dream, together we mend.

Galactic vastness, endless skies,
Where every quest begins with sighs.
In distant suns, our dreams align,
The universe sings, and we entwine.

The Light We Follow

In shadowed paths, there shines a glow,
A beacon bright, through highs and lows.
With every step, we find our way,
The light we follow leads the day.

Through tempest winds and gravel stones,
In unity, we are not alone.
A candle's flame can pierce the dark,
A spark of hope, a sacred mark.

In every heart, a light resides,
Illuminating love that bides.
Together we forge unyielding ties,
In this warm glow, our spirit flies.

As dawn ascends, our shadows fade,
With courage pure, we will not trade.
For every trial, the light will stay,
The path we walk, our guiding ray.

Whispers of Distant Luminaries

In the hush of night so deep,
Stars awaken, secrets keep.
Shooting shards of silver light,
Guiding souls through endless night.

Voices dance in cosmic glow,
Tales of time and space they sow.
Each twinkle holds a whispered dream,
Of worlds beyond, where starlight streams.

Echoes of the ages past,
Whispers in the void are cast.
Through the dark a spark will rise,
Distant truths in twilight skies.

Oh, how far the heart can soar,
To the realms we yearn for more.
Follow, follow every gleam,
In the night, pursue the dream.

In Pursuit of Celestial Dreams

Chasing shadows, bright and bold,
Through the ether, stories told.
With each step toward the stars,
We unveil our hidden scars.

Nebulae in colors bright,
Paint the canvas of the night.
In the silence, hopes ignite,
As we stretch for cosmic light.

Galaxies in endless spin,
Whispers urging us within.
Each heartbeat marks a stride we take,
In pursuit of dreams we make.

From the darkness into dawn,
In our hearts, we carry on.
Celestial paths beneath our feet,
Guiding us where stardust meets.

Journey to the Twilight Gleam

On the road to twilight's grace,
We embrace the starry space.
Every moment, echoes blend,
As the daylight starts to end.

Golden hues fade into gray,
As we wander, lose our way.
Memories in softest flight,
Guide us through the coming night.

Mountains whisper, rivers hum,
Underneath the quiet drum.
With each breath, the evening calls,
From the sky, the twilight falls.

In the stillness, shadows play,
Illuminating dreams that sway.
Twilight's gleam will light our path,
As we dance in evening's bath.

Where the Comets Sing

Beneath the arch of midnight skies,
Comets wander, free to rise.
Their tails a brush of fleeting flame,
Whispers echo, call our name.

In the darkness, music flows,
Notes of light where stardust glows.
Every galactic song we hear,
Dances softly, crystal clear.

Hearts entwined with cosmic lore,
We seek the sounds, forevermore.
In the stillness, spirits roam,
Finding comfort far from home.

Each comet tells a tale divine,
Of love, loss, and space entwined.
Where celestial notes take wing,
In that realm, where comets sing.

Milton Keynes UK
Ingram Content Group UK Ltd.
UKHW021000241024
450188UK00012B/511

9 789916 905876